For Esther J.B.
For Mum and Dad N.S.

OXFORD
UNIVERSITY PRESS

Great Clarendon Street, Oxford OX2 6DP

Oxford University Press is a department of the University of Oxford.
It furthers the University's objective of excellence in research,
scholarship, and education by publishing worldwide in

Oxford   New York

Auckland   Cape Town   Dar es Salaam   Hong Kong   Karachi
Kuala Lumpur   Madrid   Melbourne   Mexico City   Nairobi
New Delhi   Shanghai   Taipei   Toronto

With offices in

Argentina   Austria   Brazil   Chile   Czech Republic   France   Greece
Guatemala   Hungary   Italy   Japan   Poland   Portugal   Singapore
South Korea   Switzerland   Thailand   Turkey   Ukraine   Vietnam

Oxford is a registered trade mark of Oxford University Press
in the UK and in certain other countries

Arrangement and selection copyright © Jill Bennett 1999
Illustrations copyright © Nick Sharratt 1999

British Library Cataloguing in Publication Data

Data available

ISBN-13: 978-0-19-276322-8
ISBN-10: 0-19-276322-9

10 9 8 7 6 5 4 3 2

Printed in China by Imago

Acknowledgements
Every effort has been made to trace and contact copyright holders
before publication and we are grateful to all those who have granted
us permission. We apologize for any inadvertent errors and will be
pleased to rectify these at the earliest opportunity.

Ann Bonner: 'Angels' copyright © Ann Bonner 1999. Sue Cowling: 'Mary's
Cradle' and 'Star' both copyright © Sue Cowling 1999. June Crebbin: 'The
School Carol' from *The Jungle Sale* (Viking Kestrel, 1988), copyright © June
Crebbin, 1988, by permission of the author. Julia Donaldson: 'Santa
Claws' copyright © Julia Donaldson 1999. Richard Edwards: 'If' from *If
Only . . .* (Viking, 1990), copyright © Richard Edwards 1990, by permission
of the author. Michelle Magorian: 'Christmas Eve' from *Orange Paw Marks*
(Viking, 1991), copyright © Michelle Magorian 1991, by permission of
Penguin Books Ltd and the author c/o Rogers, Coleridge & White Ltd, 20
Powis Mews, London W11 1JN. Tony Mitton: 'Will There Be Snow?'
copyright © Tony Mitton 1999. Judith Nicholls: 'In Far Off Lands and
Near' and 'Ringing Bells!' both copyright Judith Nicholls 1999. Hiawyn
Oram: 'Christmas Tree Needles' from *Speaking for Ourselves* (Methuen,
1990), copyright © Hiawyn Oram 1990, by permission of the author
c/o Rogers, Coleridge & White Ltd, 20 Powis Mews, London W11 1JN.
Irene Rawnsley: 'Don't Forget the Birds' from *Rainbow Year* (Belair, 1994),
copyright © Irene Rawnsley 1994, by permission of the author.

CHRISTMAS POEMS

Collected
by
Jill
Bennett

Illustrated by
Nick
Sharratt

OXFORD
UNIVERSITY PRESS

School Carol

Deck the classrooms now with holly,
Christmas time has just begun.
Here's a reason to be jolly,
No more lessons, lots more fun!
Christmas cards and Christmas pictures
Are the order of the day;
Let us paint a red-nosed reindeer
Pulling Santa on his sleigh.

Deck the classrooms now with streamers,
Thread some snow of cotton-wool,
Spray a snow scene on the windows,
Make some crackers we can pull.
Decorate the tree with tinsel
Green and silver, red and gold,
Sew a needle-case for Grandma,
Soon the secrets can be told.

Deck the halls with sprays of holly,
Dress up in your party gear.
Here's a reason to be jolly,
No more lessons till next year!
Hurry to the Christmas Disco,
Come along and join the fun —
Dance and swing, and sing together:
Happy Christmas, everyone!

June Crebbin

In far-off lands and near

In a snow-wrapped land of the north,
far, far away,
icicle lanterns glow from firs
to celebrate the Day.

In a sun-trapped land of the south,
far, far away,
children sing on golden sands
to celebrate the Day.

In a cloud-lapped land between,
not so far away,
candles burn and carols ring
as *we* celebrate the Day.

Judith Nicholls

Will there be snow?

The cake's been iced
and the pudding's in the pot.
We've baked mince pies,
yes, we've made quite a lot.
Everything's ready.
There's two days to go.
But there's one last thing
I'm bursting to know:
Oh, will there be, will there be,
will there be snow?

The mistletoe's up
and the cards are strung.
The tree decorations
have all been hung.
Everything's ready.
There's two days to go.
But there's one last thing
I'm bursting to know:
Oh, will there be, will there be,
will there be snow?

There might be sleet
or there might be rain.
There might be wind
that rattles at the pane.
There might be a bright,
blue sky, with sun.
But when it's Christmas
what's really fun . . .
is snow, snow, thick, thick snow,
a layer of white, I love it so!

Tony Mitton

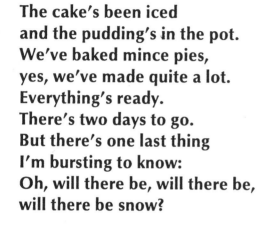

Don't forget the birds

A hungry robin
looked for food
in Laura's frosty garden,
bobbed in a fir tree
underneath the eave,

found that the branches
were full of surprises;
'An apple, nuts,
a coconut,
they must be make-believe!'

'Eat up!'
chirped a bluetit
hopped up beside him.
'Laura has remembered us.
Today is Christmas Eve!'

Irene Rawnsley

Christmas tree needles

Long and green and sharp and thin
They give us away when we've been in
Feeling our presents under the tree
The back of our jumpers are FORESTS

Hiawyn Oram

Mary's cradle

Mary stooped and patted the baby,
Stroked the top of his downy head.
How she wished she could rock the manger,
Rock that rickety manger bed.

Joseph asked, 'Is the baby hungry?'
Mary answered, 'He's just been fed.'
Joseph longed for the fine new cradle,
Fine rocking cradle in his shed.

Sue Cowling

Angels

Earth and sky,
sky and earth,
both embrace
the holy birth.

Picture angels
in that sky.
Imagine angels
there, on high.

Angel music
fills the night.
Angels wrapped
in angel light.

Candles lit
on angel chimes.
Christmas Eve.
Christmas times.

Ann Bonner

Christmas Eve

I'm trying to sleep but my eyelids won't close
And I can't help but peep, for in front of my nose
Is a long woolly stocking that's red.
If I don't fall asleep Father Christmas won't come
And he won't eat the sandwiches made by my mum,
Or put toys at the end of my bed.

Michelle Magorian

If

If I were Father Christmas
I'd deliver all my toys
By rocket ship, a sleigh's too slow
For eager girls and boys,
I'd nip down every chimney-pot
And never miss a roof,
While Rudolph worked the ship's controls
With antler tip and hoof.

Richard Edwards

Ringing bells!

One small chime
climbed from the tower ...
Follow me, follow!
And more chimes follow ...

shrill chimes, low chimes,
dancing chimes, slow chimes;

clanging chimes, ringing chimes,
pealing chimes, singing chimes;

chimes that trill, chimes that thrill,

chimes that spill themselves
over forests and rooftops
filling the earth and the skies,
filling the sky and the earth
with their Christmas message:
This is the Day of Jesus' birth!

Judith Nicholls

Santa Claws

I don't know why they're blaming me
When all I did was climb a tree
And bat a shiny silver ball.
How could I know the tree would fall?
And when those silly lights went out
They didn't have to scream and shout
And turf me out and shut the door.
Now no one loves me any more.
I'm in the kitchen by myself.
But wait! What's on that high-up shelf?
A lovely turkey, big and fat!
How nice! They *do* still love their cat.

Julia Donaldson

Star

Star came dancing
With a swoop and twist,
Spangled as a bangle
On a slave girl's wrist.

Star came pricking
Like a silver spur.
'Hurry, hurry! Fetch gold,
Frankincense and myrrh.'

Star came tugging
Like a crazy kite
Then stood still till someone
Snipped its string last night.

Sue Cowling